UNSU, SŌCHIN, NIJŪSHIHO

Unsu. Sōchin. Nijūshiho

M. Nakayama

KODANSHA USA

Kata in this volume demonstrated by Mikio Yahara, Yoshiharu Ōsaka and Tetsuhiko Asai, instructors of the Japan Karate Association.

Front cover photo by Keizō Kaneko.

Published by Kodansha USA Publishing, LLC
451 Park Avenue South, New York, NY 10016

Distributed in the United Kingdom and continental Europe
by Kodansha Europe Ltd.

ISBN: 978-1-56836-554-1
LCC 77-74829

First edition published in Japan in 1987 by Kodansha International
First US edition 2014 by Kodansha USA,
an imprint of Kodansha USA Publishing, LLC

26 25 24 23 22 8 7 6 5 4

www.kodansha.us

Dedicated
to my teacher
GICHIN FUNAKOSHI

INTRODUCTION

The past decades have seen a great increase in the popularity of karate-dō throughout the world. Among those who have taken it up have been college students and teachers, artists, businessmen and civil servants. It has come to be practiced by policemen and members of Japan's Self-defense Forces. In a number of universities, it has become a compulsory subject, and that number is increasing yearly.

Along with the increase in popularity, there have been certain unfortunate and regrettable interpretations and performances. For one thing, karate has been confused with the so-called Chinese-style boxing, and its relationship with the original Okinawan *Te* has not been suffciently understood. There are also people who have regarded it as a mere show, in which two men attack each other savagely, or the contestants battle each other as though it were a form of boxing in which the feet are used, or a man shows off his talent for breaking bricks or tiles with his head, hand or foot.

If karate is practiced solely as a fighting technique, this is cause for regret. The fundamental techniques have been developed and perfected through long years of study and practice, but to make any effective use of these techniques, the spiritual aspect of this art of self-defense must be recognized and must play the predominant role. It is gratifying to me to see that there are those who understand this, who know that karate-dō is a purely Oriental martial art, and who train with the proper attitude.

To be capable of inflicting devastating damage on any opponent with one blow of the fist or a single kick has indeed been the objective of this Okinawan martial art. But even the practitioners of old placed greater emphasis on the spiritual side of the art than on the techniques. Training means training of body and spirit, and, above all else, one should treat his opponent courteously and with the proper etiquette. It is not enough to fight with all one's might; the real objective in karate-dō is to do so for the sake of justice.

Gichin Funakoshi, a great master of karate-dō, pointed out repeatedly that the first purpose in pursuing this art is the nurturing of a sublime spirit, a spirit of humility. Simultaneously, power sufficient to destroy a ferocious wild animal with a single blow should be developed. Becoming a true follower of karate-dō is possible only when one attains perfection in these two aspects, the one spiritual, the other physical.

Karate as an art of self-defense and karate as a means of improving and maintaining health has long existed. During the past twenty years, a new aspect has been opened up and is coming to the fore. This is *sports karate*.

In sports karate, contests are held for the purpose of determining the ability of the participants. This needs emphasizing, for here again there is cause for regret. There is a tendency to be too concerned with winning contests, and those who do this neglect the practice of fundamental techniques, opting instead to attempt jiyū kumite at the earliest opportunity.

Stress on winning contests cannot help but alter the fundamental techniques a person uses and the practice he engages in. Not only that, it will result in the loss of the ability to execute strong and effective techniques, which is, after all, the unique characteristic of karate-dō. The man who begins jiyū kumite prematurely—without sufficient practice of fundamentals—will soon be surpassed by those who have trained in basic techniques long and diligently. It is, simply put, a case of haste makes waste. There is no alternative to learning and practicing basic techniques and movements step by step, stage by stage.

If karate contests are to be held, they must be conducted under suitable conditions and in the proper spirit. The desire to win a contest is counterproductive, since it leads to a lack of seriousness in learning the fundamentals. Moreover, aiming for a savage display of strength and power in a contest is totally undesirable. When this happens, courtesy toward the opponent, which is of first importance in any expression of karate, is forgotten. I believe this matter deserves a great deal of reflection and serious self-examination on the part of both instructors and students.

To explain the many and complex movements of the body, it has been my desire to present a fully illustrated, up-to-date text, based on the experience in this art I have acquired in the last five decades. This hope is being realized by the publication of this *Best Karate* series, in which earlier writings have been completely revised with the help and encouragement of my readers. This new series explains in detail what karate-dō is in language made as simple as possible, and I sincerely hope it will be useful to followers of karate-dō. I hope also that karateka in many countries will be able to understand each other better through this series of books.

WHAT KARATE-DŌ IS

Deciding who is the winner and who is the loser is not the ultimate objective. Karate-dō is a martial art for the development of character through training, so that the karateka can surmount any obstacle, tangible or intangible.

Karate-dō is an empty-handed art of self-defense in which the arms and legs are systematically trained and an enemy attacking by surprise can be controlled by a demonstration of strength like that of using actual weapons.

Karate-dō is exercise through which the karateka masters all body movements by learning to move limbs and torso backward and forward, left and right, up and down, freely and uniformly.

The techniques of karate-dō are well controlled according to the karateka's willpower and are directed at the target accurately and spontaneously.

The essence of karate techniques is *kime*. The meaning of *kime* is an explosive attack to the target using the appropriate technique and maximum power in the shortest time possible. (Long ago, there was the expression *ikken hissatsu*, meaning "to kill with one blow," but to assume from this that killing is the objective is not only incorrect but dangerous. It should be remembered that the karateka of old could practice *kime* daily and seriously by using the *makiwara*.)

Kime may be accomplished by striking, punching or kicking, but also by blocking. A technique lacking kime is never true karate. A contest is no exception, however, it is against the rules to make contact because of the danger involved.

Sun-dome means to arrest a technique just before making contact with the target (one *sun*, about three centimeters). But executing a technique without kime is not true karate, so there is the problem of reconciling kime and sun-dome. The solution is this: by establishing the target slightly in front of a person's vital point, the target can be "hit" in a controlled way with maximum power without ever making contact.

Training transforms parts of the body into weapons to be used freely and effectively. The quality necessary to accomplish this is self-control. To become a victor, one must first overcome his own self.

KATA

The *kata* of karate-dō are logical arrangements of blocking, punching, striking and kicking techniques in certain set sequences. About fifty kata ("formal exercises") are practiced nowadays, some having been passed down from generation to generation, others being of fairly recent origin.

Kata can be divided into two broad categories. In one group are those appropriate for physical development such as the strengthening of bone and muscle. Seemingly simple, they require composure for their performance and exhibit strength and dignity when performed correctly. In the second group are kata appropriate for developing fast reflexes and agility. Their lightninglike movements are suggestive of the rapid flight of the swallow. All kata require and enhance rhythm and coordination.

Training in kata is spiritual as well as physical. In his performance of kata, the karateka should exhibit boldness and confidence and at the same time humility, gentleness and a sense of decorum, thus integrating mind and body in a singular discipline. As Gichin Funakoshi frequently reminded his students, "The spirit of karate-dō is lost without courtesy."

One expression of this courtesy is the bow made at the beginning and end of each kata. The stance is *musubi-dachi*, with the arms relaxed, hands lightly touching the thighs and eyes focused straight ahead.

From the bow the karateka moves into the *kamae* of the first movement of the kata. This is always a relaxed position devoid of tenseness, especially in the shoulders and knees, and breathing should be relaxed and natural. The center of power and concentration is the *tanden*, the center of gravity. In this position, one should be full of fighting spirit and ready for any eventuality.

Being relaxed but alert also characterizes the bow completing the kata. This is called *zanshin*. In karate-dō, as in other martial arts, bringing the kata to a perfect finish is of the greatest importance.

The first technique of any kata is a block. A kata has a specific number of movements to be performed in a set order. Complexity of movements and the time required vary, but each has its own meaning and function and nothing is superfluous. Performance is carried out along the *embusen* ("performance line"), the shape of which is predetermined for each kata.

When performing kata, the karateka should imagine he is surrounded by enemies and be prepared to execute defensive and offensive techniques in any direction.

Mastery of kata is a prerequisite for advancement through *kyū* and *dan*. The kata in volumes 9, 10 and 11 of this series belong to the category of free kata, which may be selected for examination above 1st *dan*. They are of a fairly advanced level, and successful performance depends on having first mastered fundamentals, basic techniques and the required kata.

Important Points

Since the effects of practice are cumulative, train every day, even if only for a few minutes. When performing a kata, keep calm; never rush through the movements. You must always be aware of the correct timing of each movement. If a particular kata proves difficult, give it more attention, and always keep in mind the relationship between kata practice and kumite. (*See* Vols. 3 and 4.)

Specific points in performance are:

1. *Correct order.* The number and sequence of movements is predetermined. All must be performed.
2. *Beginning and end.* The kata must begin and end at the same spot on the *embusen*. This requires practice.
3. *Meaning of each movement.* Each movement, defensive or offensive, must be clearly understood and fully expressed. This is also true of a kata as a whole, since each one has its own characteristics.
4. *Awareness of the target.* The karateka must know what the target is and precisely when to execute a technique.
5. *Rhythm and timing.* Rhythm must be appropriate to the kata and the body must be flexible, never overstrained. Always keep in mind three factors: correct use of power, swiftness or slowness in executing a technique, and the stretching and contraction of muscles.
6. *Proper breathing.* Breathing should adjust to changing situations, but basically inhale when blocking, exhale when executing a finishing technique, and inhale and exhale while executing successive techniques.

Closely related to breathing is the *kiai* coming in the middle or at the end of the kata, at moments of maximum tension. By exhaling very sharply and tensing the abdomen, extra power can be imparted to the muscles.

Standardization

The basic Heian and Tekki kata and the free kata from Bassai to Jion are all the essentially important Shōto-kan kata. In 1948, disciples from Keio, Waseda and Takushoku universities met with Master Gichin Funakoshi at Waseda University. Their purpose was to form a viewpoint for the unification of the kata, which in the period after the war were subject to varied individual and subjective interpretations. The kata as presented in *Best Karate* embody the criteria for standardization established at that time.

Rhythm

UNSU

1 2・3 4 5 6 7 8・9 10・11 12・13 14・15 16 17
18 19 20 21 22・23・24 25 26・27・28 29 30・31 32・33
34 35 36 37・38 39 40 41 42 43 44 45 46 47・48

SŌCHIN

1 2 3・4 5 6 7 8・9 10 11 12 13・14 15・16 17・18
19 20 21 22 23 24・25・26・27・28 29・30 31 32 33 34
35 36 37 38 39・40

NIJŪSHIHO

1 2・3 4・5 6・7 8・9 10 11・12 13 14・15 16 17
18・19・20 21 22 23・24 25 26 27 28 29・30
31 32 33

slow, increasingly strong
suddenly apply power
slow, quiet and strong
strong and slow
continuous, fast
one continuous action
kiai
powerfully

Unsu

From shizen-tai move slowly to kamae. Arms slant diagonally downward, backs of fists upward.

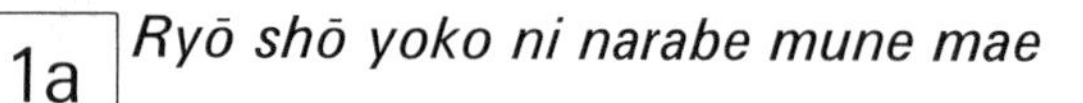

1a *Ryō shō yoko ni narabe mune mae*

Outer edges of hands brought together in front of chest Slowly raise hands in front of chest. Elbows and wrists are bent.

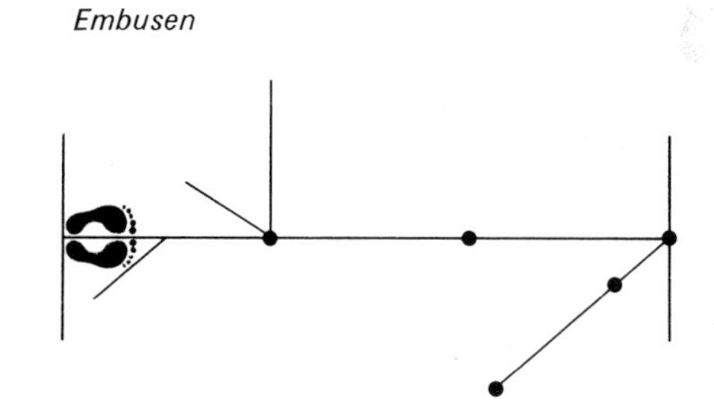

Embusen

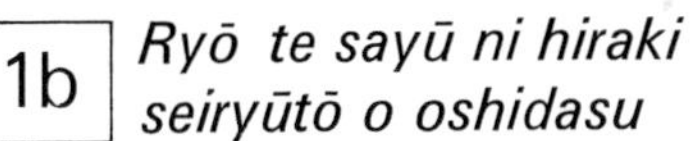

1b Ryō te sayū ni hiraki seiryūtō o oshidasu

Heisoku-dachi

Open hands to sides, push ox jaw hands outward Straighten elbows, extend arms out to the sides. Make ox jaw hands with wrists bent, palms facing forward.

2 *Ryō te chūdan keitō uke (Ryō keitō wa hiji yori sukoshi hiraki gimi ni)*

Middle level chicken-head wrist blocks/Hands slightly farther apart than the elbows Slide the right big toe forward in a clockwise semicircle. Lower and raise hands

3 *Migi hitosashiyubi gedan ippon nukite Hidari te sono mama*

Right index-finger spear hand to lower level/Left hand as it is While keeping the right upper arm and elbow fixed, snap the forearm downward, then quickly bring

Migi mae neko ashi-dachi

with the wrists bent. Elbows are aligned with sides of body; tighten armpits.

Migi mae neko ashi-dachi

it back using the elbow snap.

4 *Ryō te chūdan keitō uke no mama*

Middle level chicken-head wrist blocks as they are Slide the left big toe forward in a counterclockwise arc.

5 *Hidari hitosashiyubi gedan ippon nukite* *Migi te sono mama*

Left index-finger spear hand to lower level/Right hand as it is Use the elbow snap to retract the spear hand.

Hidari mae neko ashi-dachi

Hidari mae neko ashi-dachi

6

Ryō te chūdan keitō uke no mama

Middle level chicken-head wrist blocks as they are

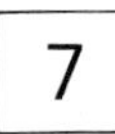

7

Migi hitosashiyubi gedan ippon nukite
Hidari te sono mama

Right index-finger spear hand to lower level/Left hand as it is · Use snap of elbow to retract striking arm.

Migi mae neko ashi-dachi

Migi mae neko ashi-dachi

8 *Hidari chūdan tate shutō uke*

Left middle level vertical sword hand block With right foot as pivot, slide left foot out to the left.

9 *Migi chūdan gyaku-zuki*

Hidari zenkutsu-dachi

Right middle level reverse punch Without lifting feet, shift from rooted stance to front stance. Movements 8 and 9 are done as one continuous action.

10 *Migi chūdan tate shutō uke*

Hidari ashi mae fudō-dachi

Migi ashi mae fudō-dachi

Right middle level vertical sword hand block With left foot as pivot, rotate hips to the right.

11 *Hidari chūdan gyaku-zuki*

Left middle level reverse punch Without lifting feet, shift from rooted stance to front stance. Movements 10 and 11 are done as one continuous action.

12 *Hidari chūdan tate shutō uke*

Left middle level vertical sword hand block With right foot as pivot, rotate hips to the left and slide left foot to the front.

Migi zenkutsu-dachi

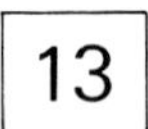

Hidari ashi mae fudō-dachi

13 *Migi chūdan gyaku-zuki*

Hidari zenkutsu-dachi

Right middle level reverse punch Without lifting feet, shift to front stance.

14 *Migi chūdan tate shutō uke*

Right middle level vertical sword hand block With left foot as pivot, rotate hips to the right to face in the opposite direction.

16 *Hidari ashi mawashi-geri* *Jōtai migi naname ni fuseru/Migi hiza kaikomu*

Left roundhouse kick/Lie flat, torso diagonally to the right/Fold right knee Bend right knee and drop sideways to the ground, immediately executing a left round-

15 *Hidari chūdan gyaku-zuki*

Migi ashi mae fudō-dachi

Migi zenkutsu-dachi

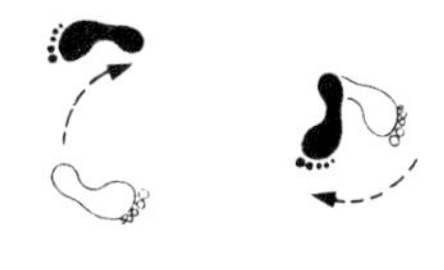

Left middle level reverse punch Without lifting feet, shift to front stance.

house kick. Place both hands (elbows bent) in line with the position of the feet.

17 *Migi ashi mawashi-geri* *Jōtai hidari naname ni fuseru/Hidari hiza kaikomu*

Right roundhouse kick/Lie flat, torso diagonally to the left/Fold left knee Place left knee ahead of right knee and straighten elbows to raise torso. Both kicks are

executed along a single line but in opposite directions.

18 *Ryō te sayū ni chūdan seiryūtō-zuki*

Middle level ox jaw hand strikes to both sides Use the left foot for support, stand up and slide right foot slowly forward (three seconds). Finish hand and foot move-

Hidari chūdan keitō uke
Migi gedan teishō yoko uke

Left middle level chicken-head wrist block/Right side downward palm heel block Bring right foot alongside left foot and immediately slide left foot one step forward.

Kiba-dachi

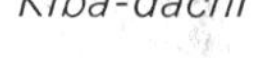

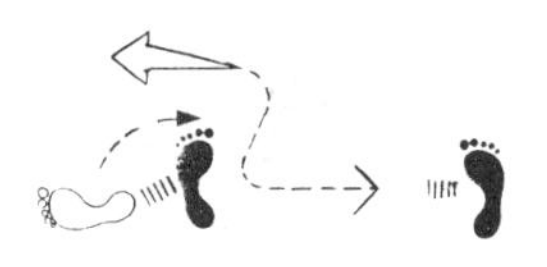

ments at the same time.

Hidari zenkutsu-dachi

20 *Migi chūdan keitō uke* *Hidari gedan teishō yoko uke*

Right middle level chicken-head wrist block/Left side downward palm heel block
Pull left foot alongside right foot and immediately slide right foot one step forward.

21 *Hidari jōdan haitō uchi*

Left upper level ridge hand strike Stance does not change.

Migi zenkutsu-dachi

Migi zenkutsu-dachi

22 *Hidari mae-geri (Hidari shō saki o keru)*
Hidari te sono mama

Left front kick (beyond extended left hand)/Left hand as it is

23 *Migi jōdan soto uke*

Right upper level block, outside inward After kicking, bring left foot beside right knee. Immediately rotate hips rightward with right foot as pivot. Take right front

Migi ashi-dachi

Migi ashi-dachi

stance (facing in opposite direction) as left kicking foot returns to the ground. Execute a right upper level block, outside inward.

24 *Hidari chūdan gyaku-zuki*

Migi zenkutsu-dachi

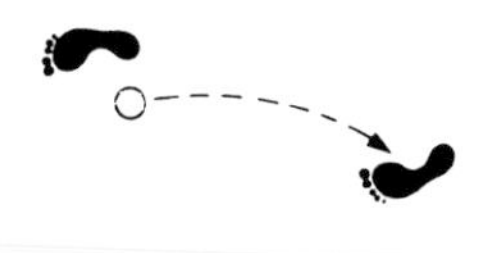

Left middle level reverse punch At same time right front stance is assumed, execute a reverse punch. Do Movements 22, 23 and 24 consecutively.

25 *Migi jōdan haitō uchi*

Right upper level ridge hand strike With right foot as pivot, rotate hips to the left. Take the front stance facing to the front.

Hidari zenkutsu-dachi

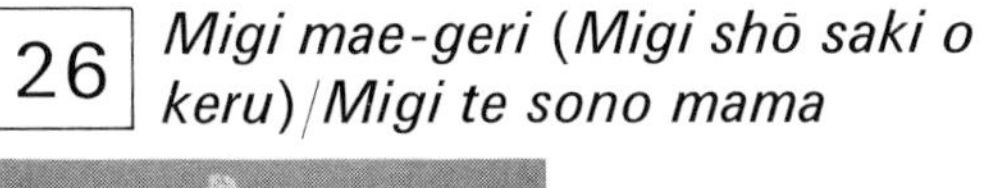

26 *Migi mae-geri (Migi shō saki o keru)/Migi te sono mama*

Migi ashi-dachi

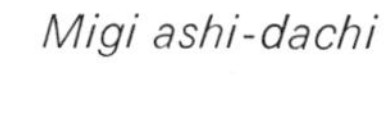

Right front kick (beyond extended right hand) /Right hand as it is

27 *Hidari jōdan soto uke*

Left upper level block, outside inward Return kicking foot to left knee and immediately pivot to the left to reverse direction. Execute the block while moving

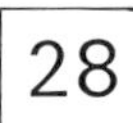

28 *Migi chūdan gyaku-zuki*

Hidari zenkutsu-dachi

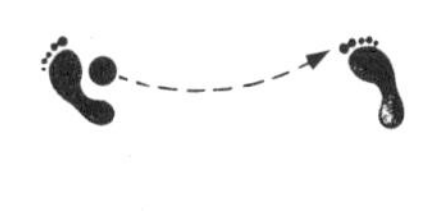

Right middle level reverse punch At the same time the left front stance is taken, execute a right reverse punch. Do Movements 26, 27 and 28 consecutively.

29 *Ryō ken naname shita ni kamaeru*

Hidari ashi-dachi

into the left front stance.

Heisoku-dachi

Both fists diagonally downward at sides kamae Slowly bring left foot back to right foot.

30 *Migi shō jōdan kensei*

Right hand upper level feint First slide left foot diagonally to the left. Raise and lower left palm, buinging it back toward left hip; raise right palm high and then

31 *Migi gedan-zuki*

30-31. Migi zenkutsu-dachi

Right downward punch Execute the punch while sliding right foot forward.

bring it down. Movement of hands resembles rope climbing.

32 *Hidari gedan uke-zuki*

Hidari zenkutsu-dachi

Left downward block-punch With right foot as pivot, rotate hips to the left into left front stance.

33 *Migi gedan uke-zuki*

Right downward block-punch With left foot as pivot, rotate hips to the right into right front stance.

34 *Hidari chūdan tate shutō uke*

Migi zenkutsu-dachi

Hidari ashi mae fudō-dachi

Left middle level vertical sword hand block With right foot as pivot, rotate hips to the left and take left rooted stance.

35 *Chūdan teishō hasami uke*

Middle level palm heel scissors block Without lifting feet, shift from rooted stance to front stance.

36 *Ryō shō tsukamiyose* *Migi gedan mae kekomi*

Grasping-pulling with both hands/Right downward thrust kick While grasping and pulling opponent with both hands, thrust kick with the right ankle going dia-

Hidari zenkutsu-dachi

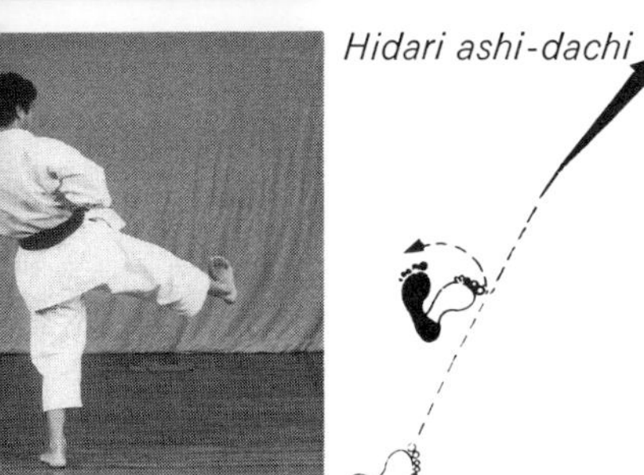

Hidari ashi-dachi

gonally downward.

37 *Hidari chūdan gyaku-zuki*

Left middle level reverse punch Execute punch while taking stance.

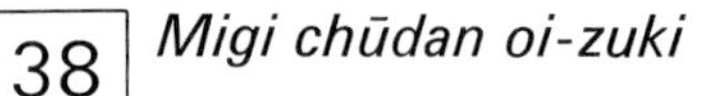

38 *Migi chūdan oi-zuki*

Right middle level lunge punch Movements 37 and 38 are one continuous action.

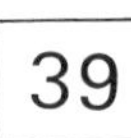

39 *Migi gedan-barai*

Right downward block With left foot as pivot, rotate hips to the left and take the straddle-leg stance.

37-38. *Migi zenkutsu-dachi*

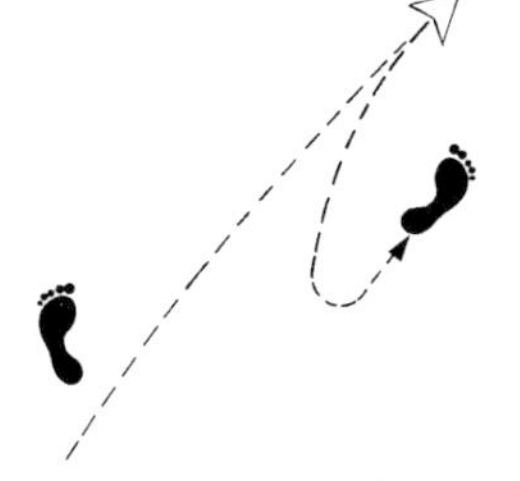

Kiba-dachi

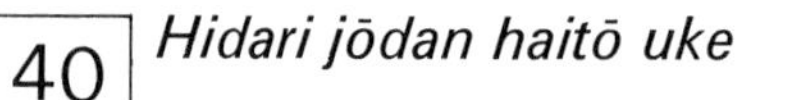

40 *Hidari jōdan haitō uke*

Left upper level ridge hand block The stance does not change.

41 *Hidari shutō gedan-barai*

Left downward sword hand block With right foot as pivot, rotate hips to the right and take the straddle-leg stance.

Kiba-dachi

42 *Migi jōdan haitō uke*

Right upper level ridge hand block The stance does not change.

43 *Hidari chūdan gyaku-zuki*

Left middle level reverse punch The stance does not change.

44a Hidari chūdan tate shutō uke
Ittan hidari shō o kōhō e

Kō hidari muki

Left middle level vertical sword hand block/Left palm first faces back (*back of fist facing left*) With right foot as pivot, rotate hips to the left. Move the left hand

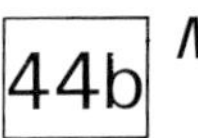

Migi chūdan mikazuki-geri

Right middle level crescent kick

Hidari ashi-dachi

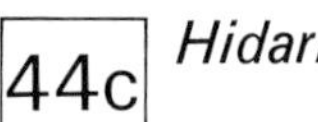

Hidari ashi mae fudō-dachi

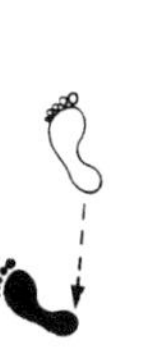

slowly in a circle while turning backward.

44c *Hidari ushiro e kekomi*

Back thrust kick With left foot as pivot, deliver crescent kick to the back with right foot. Using the same momentum, spin 360° in the air and while landing, deliver a

back thrust kick to the front. When landing, take a crouching position with the right foot forward. After the crescent kick, tuck right knee as high up on the

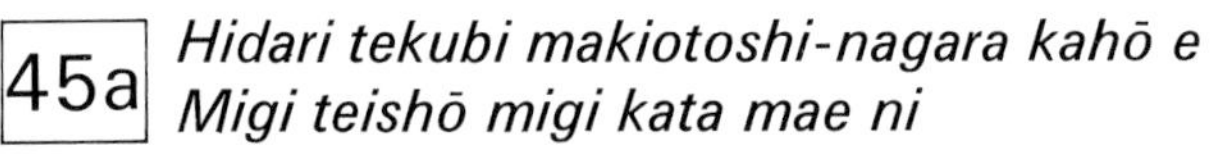

45a *Hidari tekubi makiotoshi-nagara kahō e Migi teishō migi kata mae ni*

Left wrist downward hooking block/Right palm heel in front of right shoulder
Cross the right hand over the left hand. Move hands slowly while turning them.

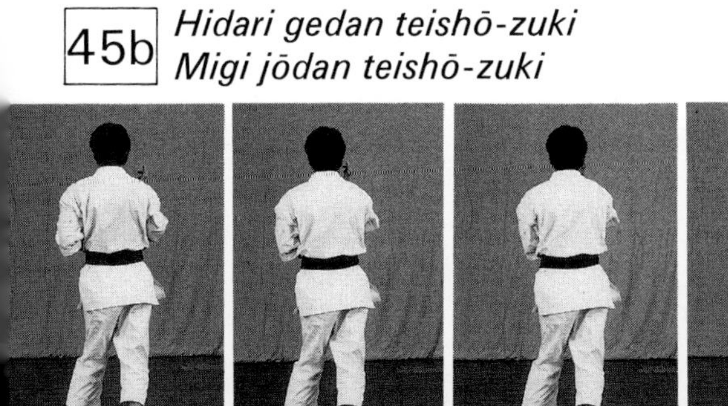

body as possible. Right before landing, deliver a thrust kick backward. At this time, the body is a straight line facing the ground.

45b *Hidari gedan teishō-zuki* *Migi jōdan teishō-zuki*

Hidari ashi mae sanchin-dachi

Left lower level palm heel punch/Right upper level palm heel punch Gradually thrust left palm downward. right palm upward, punch on a vertical line.

46a *Migi tekubi makiotoshi-nagara kahō e Hidari teishō hidari kata mae ni*

Right wrist downward hooking block/Left palm heel in front of left shoulder

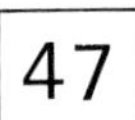

47 *Hidari jōdan age-uke*

Left upper level rising block With right foot as pivot, rotate hips to the left, face the front and take the rooted stance with left foot forward.

46b Migi gedan teishō-zuki / Hidari jōdan teishō-zuki

Right lower level palm heel punch/Left upper level palm heel punch Do Movement 46 slowly.

48 *Migi chūdan gyaku-zuki*

Naore

Hidari zenkutsu-dachi

Right middle level reverse punch Without lifting feet, shift from rooted stance to front stance.

Heisoku-dachi

Lower fists to slant diagonally downward to either side (same as initial kamae). Slowly take shizen-tai to finish the kata.

Shizen-tai hachinoji-dachi

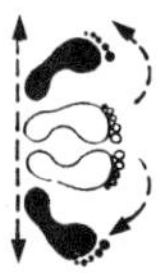

UNSU: IMPORTANT POINTS

Though not always visible to the naked eye, clouds undergo incessant transformations. So, too, does this kata, which takes its name—"Cloud Hands"—from this phenomenon. In response to the moves of adversaries, there are high and low jumps, slides, feints and provocations, using all parts of the body as weapons and developing, especially, lightness and quickness, timing, rhythm and strategic skills.

One of the unique features of this kata is the combination going from chicken-head wrist block to one-finger spear hand counterattack. Others are the skillful use of kicks delivered in a number of directions.

Unsu is very popular at the present time, but to avoid looking like a scarecrow trying to dance, the karateka must have first mastered the basic kata, particularly Heian, Kankū, Empi and Jion.

1. Movement 1. From a relaxed position with the hands at the sides, raise both hands and block the punch to the jaw with the palm heels upward and wrists bent. Turn your wrists over, grasp your adversary's punching arm, and pull to the side, throwing him off balance. Another use of this technique is to push away simultaneous attacks from the sides by lowering the hips and using the ox jaw hand. In such a case, keep the palms to the front (not to the sides).

2. Movemeuts 2/3. Drop the ox jaw hands to the sides and use chicken head wrists to block the adversary's punching arm inside outward. Do this while sliding the right foot forward into the cat leg stance, dropping the hips low enough to provide stability.

3. Movement 7. After the chicken head wrist block, counterattack to the solar plexus or thigh with the one-knuckle fist. Use the snap of the forearm with the elbow as the center of the arc. The block should be executed with the chicken head wrist dropping downward and the arm straightening to describe a semicircle. Here, too, use the snap of the elbow.

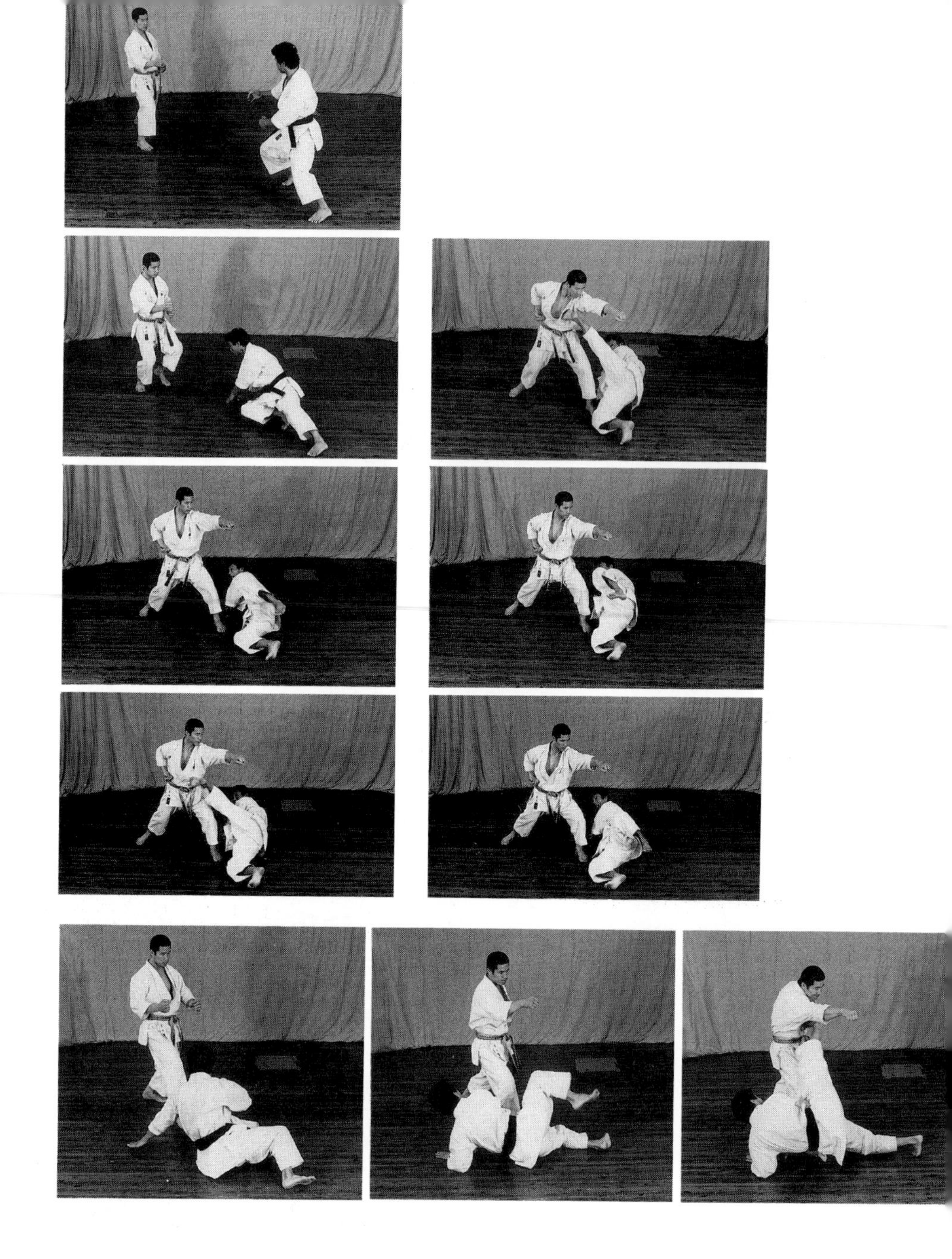

4. Movements 16/17. When falling, angle the body to one side (about 45°. Fall on left knee, right knee, both hands, right elbow, and then deliver the kick with the left foot. Immediately after returning the kicking foot, shift the upper body to the opposite side. Do this straightening the right elbow to raise the body and putting the left kicking foot diagonally ahead of the right knee. Put both hands on the ground first, then the left elbow. Both kicks are directed at a target to the front.

5. Movements 31/32. If you are face to face with an adversary and standing still, you can raise your sword hand high and when he focuses his attention on it, make a fist and punch downward. Reversing direction, block the right foot of the attacker behind you with your left arm. Again reverse direction and attack the lower level with a downward strike-block with the right fist.

Here the hands are used like lures to test your opponent's reaction. Study the course and speed of the hand movements that are most effective for this purpose.

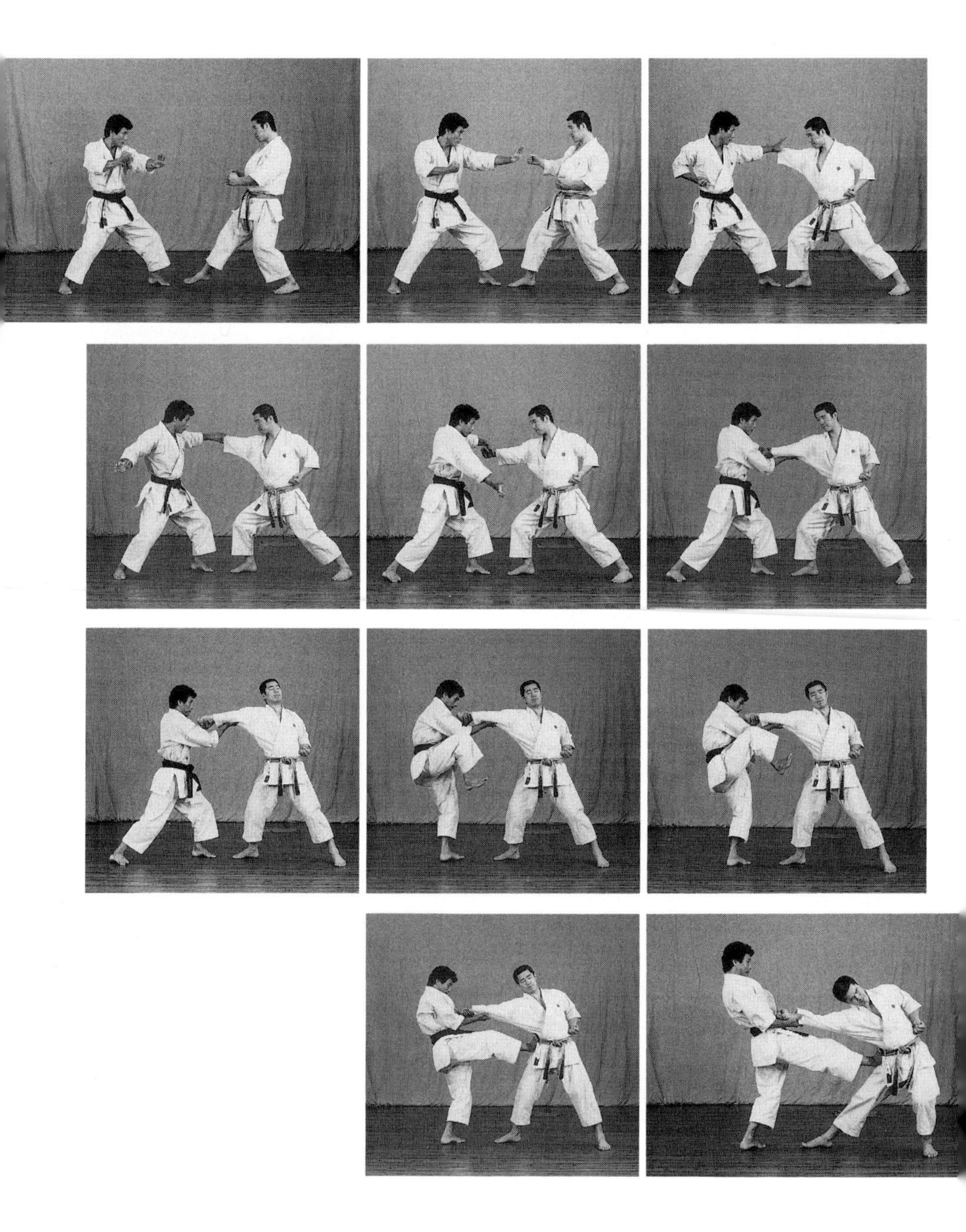

6. Movements 35/36. While using the vertical sword hand to divert the punching arm to the side, grasp the wrist and pull downward, simultaneously strike upward with the right palm heel. You can also raise the right knee high and thrust kick downward while bending his elbow back. These techniques. are very strong and decisive.

Sōchin

Yōi

1 *Migi gedan uke* *Hidari jōdan age-uke*

Right lower level block/Left upper level rising block From shizen-tai slide right foot forward for rooted stance while bringing right fist downward for the block.

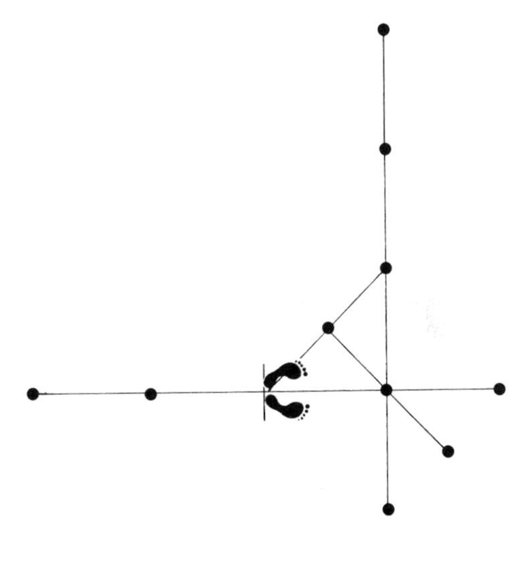

Embusen

Migi fudō-dachi

Rotate left fist while raising it. Hand and foot movements must be coordinated with the hands' crossing in front of chest and their gradual tensing.

Migi chūdan tate shutō uke

Right middle level vertical sword hand block Slide left foot forward for rooted stance and execute right middle level block slowly. Increase tension gradually.

Hidari chūdan oi-zuki

Hidari fudō-dachi

Left middle level lunge punch

4 *Migi chūdan gyaku-zuki*

Hidari fudō-dachi

Right middle level reverse punch

Hidari fudō-dachi

5 *Migi ken sokumen jōdan uchi uke* *Hidari ken sokumen gedan uke*

Hidari kōkutsu-dachi

Right upper level inside-outward block to right side/Left lower level block to left side With right foot as pivot, rotate hips to the left. Block to upper and lower levels.

6 *Migi ken gedan uke* *Hidari ken jōdan uke*

Right lower level block/Left upper level block Slide right foot into right rooted stance. Do upper and lower level blocks simultaneously and strongly.

7 *Migi chūdan tate shutō uke*

Right middle level vertical sword hand block Slide left foot another step forward. Finish hand and foot movements at the same time, slowly but powerfully.

8 *Hidari chūdan oi-zuki*

Hidari fudō-dachi

Left middle level lunge punch

9 *Migi chūdan gyaku-zuki*

Hidari fudō-dachi

Right middle level reverse punch

10 *Migi ken sokumen jōdan uchi uke* *Hidari ken sokumen gedan uke*

Right upper level inside-outward block to right side/Left lower level block to left side With right foot as pivot, rotate hips to the left to quickly face in the opposite

11 *Migi ken gedan uke* *Hidari ken jōdan uke*

Right lower level block/Left upper level block

Migi kōkutsu-dachi

direction in the right back stance.

Migi fudō-dachi

12 *Migi chūdan tate shutō uke*

Right middle level vertical sword hand block Slide left foot a step forward slowly but strongly, gradually increasing power.

13 *Hidari chūdan oi-zuki*

Hidari fudō-dachi

Left middle level lunge punch

14 *Migi chūdan gyaku-zuki*

Hidari fudō-dachi

Right middle level reverse punch

15 *Hidari jōdan yoko uraken uchi*
Hidari chūdan yoko keage

Left upper level back-fist strike to side/Left middle level snap kick to side Pull back the kicking foot as if to make it come out of the right knee.

16 *Migi chūdan hiji ate (Hidari shō ni ateru)*

Right middle level elbow strike to the front As kicking foot lands, take left rooted stance and strike right elbow against left palm.

18 *Hidari chūdan mae hiji-ate (Migi shō ni ateru)*

Left middle level elbow strike to the front (Strike right palm)

17 *Migi jōdan yoko uraken uchi* / *Migi chūdan yoko keage*

Right upper level back-fist strike to side/Right middle level kick to side With left foot as pivot, rotate hips to the right. While turning, deliver the snap kick to the side.

19 *Migi chūdan shutō uke*

Right middle level sword hand block With left foot as pivot, rotate hips to the right. Execute the sword hand block while turning the head.

Left middle level sword hand block Slide left foot diagonally forward for the stance.

Right middle level sword hand block

21 *Hidari chūdan shutō uke*

Left middle level sword hand block With right foot as pivot, rotate hips to the left.
Execute the block to the left side.

23 *Migi chūdan shutō uke*

Right middle level sword hand block

24 *Hidari chūdan shutō uke*

Migi kōkutsu-dachi

Left middle level sword hand block Slide left foot forward.

26 *Ryō te sono mama Hidari ashi chūdan mae-geri*

Both hands as they are/Left middle level front kick

25 Migi jōdan yoko nukite Hidari shō chūdan osae-uke

Migi kōkutsu-dachi

Right upper level horizontal spear hand/Middle level pressing block with left palm
Slide feet forward while keeping right back stance.

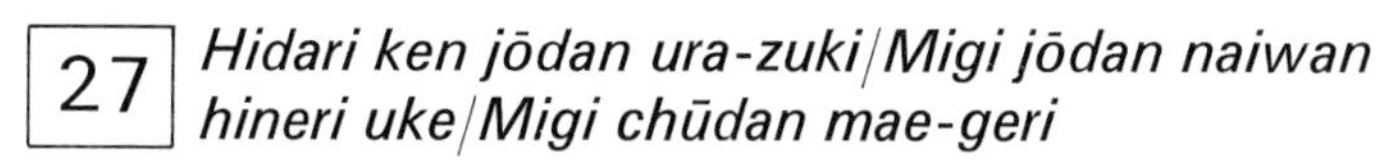

27 Hidari ken jōdan ura-zuki/Migi jōdan naiwan hineri uke/Migi chūdan mae-geri

Migi ashi-dachi

Upper level close punch with left fist/Right upper level inner forearm twisting block/Right middle level front kick

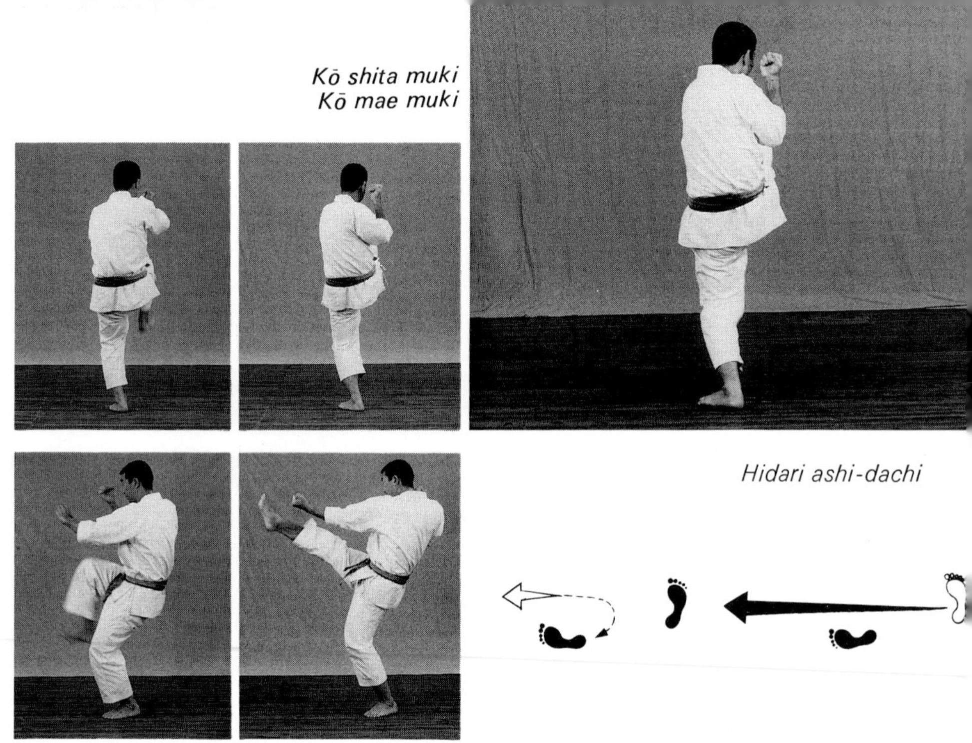

Immediately after left kicking leg lands, deliver front kick with right leg, simultaneously raise right forearm while twisting it rightward for block.

29 *Migi jōdan mikazuki-geri* *Migi shō kōhō e nobasu*

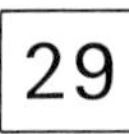

Right upper level crescent kick/Extend right hand to the back With left foot as pivot, rotate hips to the left. While turning, drive right foot against left palm.

28 *Migi jōdan ura-zuki* *Hidari jōdan naiwan hineri uke*

Kō shita muki
Kō mae muki

Migi fudō-dachi

Upper level close punch with right fist/Left upper level inner forearm twisting block
As kicking leg returns, execute block and punch with simultaneous kime.

Kō hidari muki

Hidari ashi-dachi

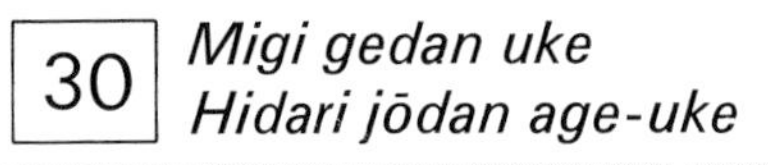

30 *Migi gedan uke* *Hidari jōdan age-uke*

Right lower level block/Left upper level rising block Bring right kicking foot down to the front and take rooted stance. Swing right fist down in a wide motion from

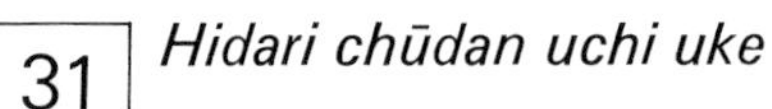

31 *Hidari chūdan uchi uke*

Left middle level inside-outward block Bring left foot diagonally to the front with right foot as support.

Migi fudō-dachi

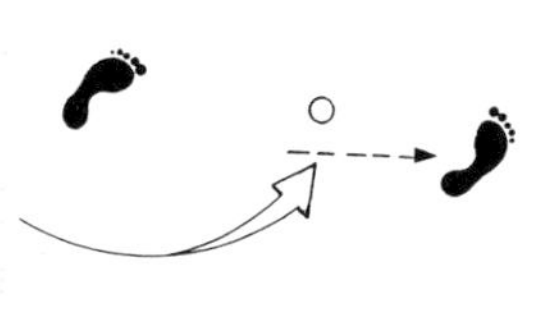

above the head. Cross hands in front of chest and execute upper and lower level blocks as if strongly pulling the hands apart.

Hidari fudō-dachi

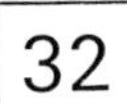

Migi chūdan oi-zuki

Right middle level lunge punch Slide right foot forward and execute the lunge punch while taking the rooted stance.

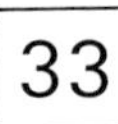

Migi chūdan uchi uke

Right middle level inside-outward block With left foot as pivot, rotate hips to the right. Slide right foot diagonally to the right front while executing the block.

Migi fudō-dachi

Migi fudō-dachi

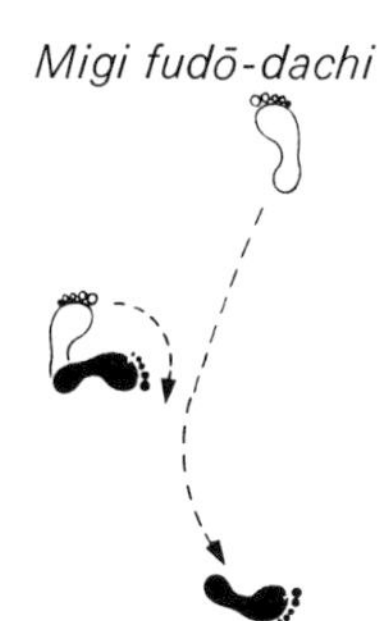

Hidari chūdan oi-zuki

Left middle level lunge punch Slide left foot forward.

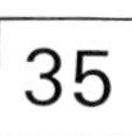

Hidari chūdan uchi uke

Left middle level inside-outward block With right foot as pivot, rotate hips to the left, shifting left foot to the left for the rooted stance.

Hidari fudō-dachi

Hidari fudō-dachi

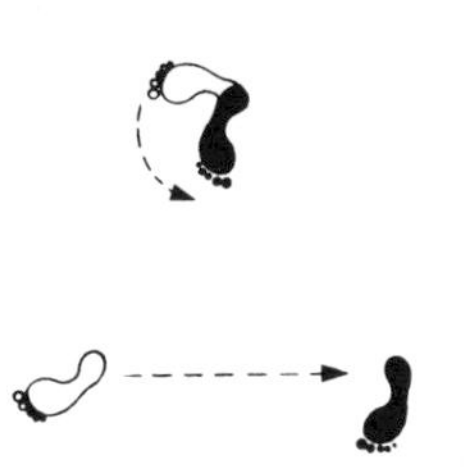

36 *Migi chūdan uchi uke (Jōtai gyaku hanmi)*

Hidari fudō-dachi

Right middle level inside-outward block Keeping the same stance, take reverse half-front facing position. Block inside outward with right fist.

38 *Hidari chūdan-zuki*
Migi ken migi chichi mae ni kamaeru

Left middle level punch/Right fist in front of right nipple kamae Bring right kicking foot back to its former position and execute left middle level punch. With-

37 *Shisei sono mama* *Migi chūdan mae-geri*

Posture as it is/Right middle level front kick

drawal of kicking leg, punch and withdrawal of right fist must be done simultaneously and slowly but strongly. Increase tension gradually.

39 *Migi chūdan gyaku-zuki*

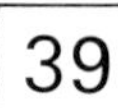

Hidari fudō-dachi

Right middle level reverse punch Movements 39 and 40 are consecutive punches.

40 *Hidari chūdan oi-zuki*

Left middle level lunge punc

Naore

Hidari fudō-dachi

Withdraw left hand slowly to return to shizen-tai.

Shizen-tai

SŌCHIN: IMPORTANT POINTS

In Sōchin we find grandeur, strength and stable power. So much use is made of the solidly stable rooted stance (*fudō-dachi*) that the stance is often referred to as the Sōchin stance.

When defense is called for, the rooted stance provides a strong basis for resisting attacks from the front, the rear or either side. The characteristics of the kata are manifested best when it is performed slowly, thereby bringing out a certain awesomeness and power. The relatively slow pace means that muscles are often brought very gradually from a state of full relaxation to full tension. Some movements, however, require an instantaneous production of muscular power. One of the benefits of the kata is the nurturing of a keen sense of timing that allows repeated attacks without giving the opponent time for a counterattack.

A great deal of karate skill can be fostered by these magnificent techniques, which help to develop the imperturbability of mind necessary for the way of the martial arts and for life itself.

1. Movement 1. The left rising block is executed while sliding the right foot forward to close the distance. Start the downward block against the opponent's kick at the same time. The basic downward block starts at the left shoulder and goes diagonally down to the right. In this application, effective against a kick at close quarters, strike straight down with the right fist.

2. Movements 2/3. Lunge punch following vertical sword hand block. For the block, straighten the elbow and bend the wrist well so the palm is facing forward. Swing the hand wide from the left side and block with the ox jaw or the edge of the hand.

3. Movements 5/6. After simultaneous upper and lower level blocks to the sides, slide the right foot forward and take a low rooted stance. At the same time, swing the right fist down from above the head to defend against the next attack. In this case, the attacker's left kick is blocked from the inside, his right kicking leg from the outside.

4. Movements 24/25. In the right back stance, block with the left sword hand, then maintain the stance while sliding forward for a right spear hand counterattack to the throat. Strike down his middle level punch with the left palm heel at the same time. Use the left foot for a fast kick to the lower abdomen or solar plexus. It is most important that the sliding movement of the feet be smooth.

Note that the kick is delivered with the forward foot. After shortening the distance, hold the knee high and close to the body and kick with a strong sharp snapping action.

6. Movements 28/30. Against an upper level attack coming from behind, rotate the hips to the left and strike the opponent's punching arm with a right crescent kick. While bringing the kicking leg down to the front, swing the right fist down in a big arc from overhead to strike block his lower level attack. To execute the crescent kick, the right knee is held high and close to the body without changing the height of the hips.

5. Movements 27/28. After kicking, execute a twisting block with the right wrist against the assailant's punching arm simultaneously with a right front kick to his solar plexus. Returning to the right rooted stance, rotate to the left and twist-block his punch from the inside with the wrist. Counterattack at the same time with a right close punch to the jaw or throat. Do not pause between techniques, which will be effective only if each one is executed with precision.

7. Movements 35/38. Successively block the opponent's right middle level lunge punch with the left forearm, inside outward, and his left reverse punch with a right forearm block, inside outward. Immediately counterattack with a snap kick to the solar plexus. While bringing back the kicking leg, the left fist can be used for a body blow. To correctly make use of the blocking arms, rotate the hips without moving the feet.

Nijūshiho

Yōi

1 *Hidari shō chūdan osae*

Middle level press-down with left palm Bring right foot back, slide left foot toward right foot for back stance. Slowly bring left palm back toward body. Increase tension

Shizen-tai

Embusen

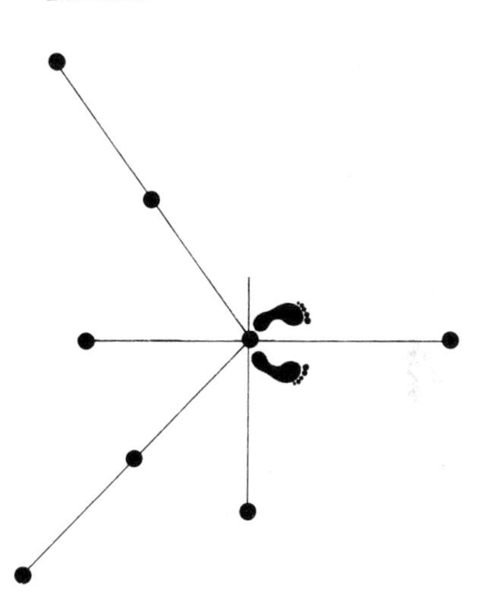

Migi kōkutsu-dachi

gradually.

2 *Migi chūdan gyaku-zuki* *Hidari shō migi hiji ue ni soeru*

Right middle level reverse punch/Left palm on right elbow Keep the stance, slide both feet forward, and execute right middle level reverse punch. Thrust punch, al-

3 *Hidari chūdan mae hiji-ate*

Left middle level elbow strike to front Slide left foot forward first, then right foot. Toes to the front and weight slightly more on left foot.

Migi kōkutsu-dachi

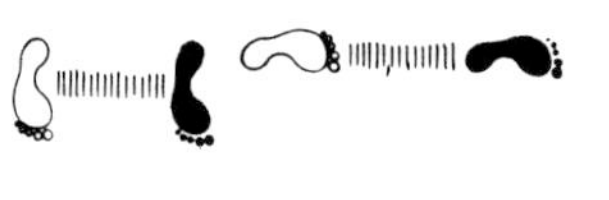

most brushing right forearm against left palm.

Hidari shizen-tai

Movement 1 is slow, Movement 2 fast and Movement 3 slow. Changes in tempo should always be smooth.

4 *Ryō ken ryō koshi kamae*

Fist at sides of body kamae With left foot as pivot, rotate hips to the right. While turning, swing both fists above the head and downward, crossing them. Pull fists

5 *Ryō ken awase-zuki* (*Migi ken jōdan, hidari ken chūdan*)

Migi mae sanchin-dachi

U punch (*Right fist upper level, left fist middle level*)

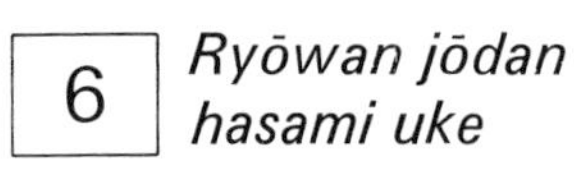

6 *Ryōwan jōdan hasami uke*

Migi mae sanchin-dachi

strongly to take kamae.

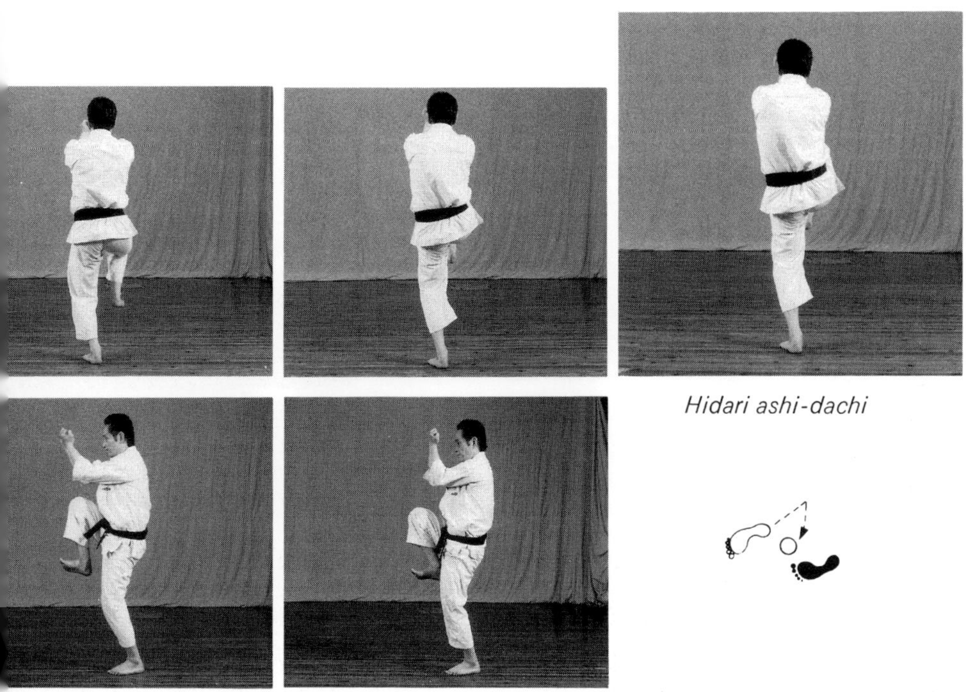
Hidari ashi-dachi

Upper level scissors block with both arms Raise right leg, simultaneously bringing the forearms together vertically in front of the face, backs of hands forward.

7 *Ryō ken chūdan kakiwake*

Middle level reverse wedge block Lower right foot to take right front stance and cross fists in front of the chest for reverse wedge block. Do slowly.

8 *Hidari jōdan age-uke*

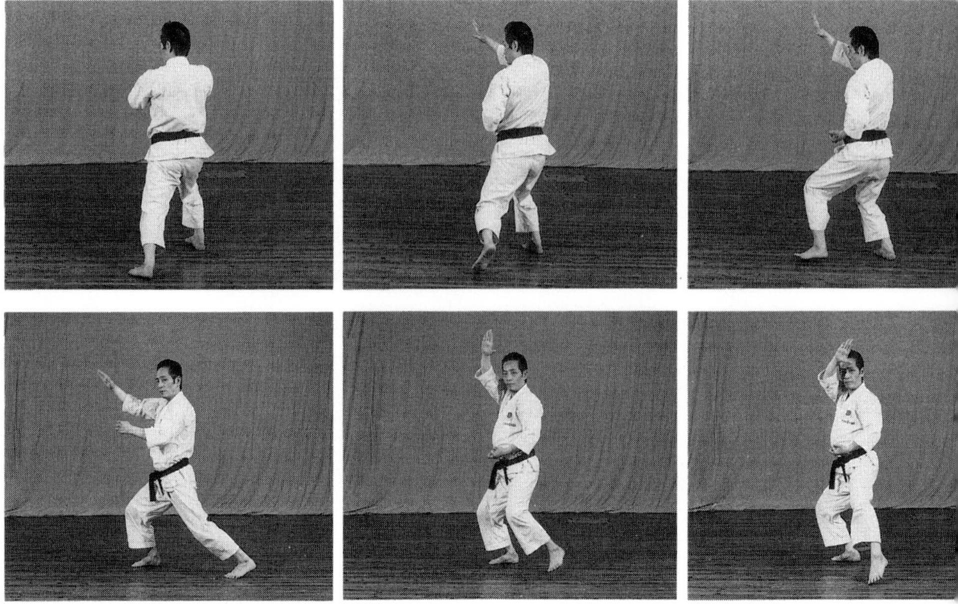

Left upper level rising block With right foot as pivot, rotate hips to the left and slide left foot to left side.

Migi zenkutsu-dachi

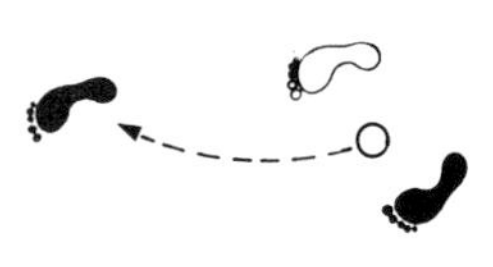

Hidari zenkutsu-dachi

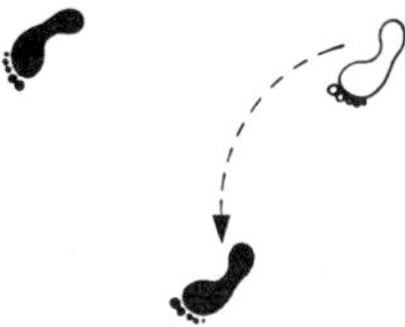

9 *Migi jōdan tate hiji-ate*

Right upper level upward elbow strike Rotate hips to the left to take reverse half-front facing position.

10 *Migi chūdan kake shutō uke*

Right middle level hooking sword hand block Rotate hips to the right to take straddle-leg stance.

Hidari zenkutsu-dachi

Kiba-dachi

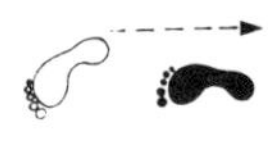

11 *Migi ken migi koshi*
Migi chūdan yoko kekomi

Right fist at right side/Right middle level side thrust kick Pull right fist strongly to right side of the body. The hips must be well set while kicking.

13 *Hidari chūdan kake shutō uke*

Left middle level hooking sword hand block

12 *Hidari chūdan-zuki*

Left middle level punch

Kiba-dachi

14 *Hidari ken hidari koshi* *Hidari chūdan yoko kekomi*

Left fist at left side/Left middle level side thrust kick Keep hips in the same position. This side kick is the reverse of the returning wave kick (*nami-gaeshi*) in

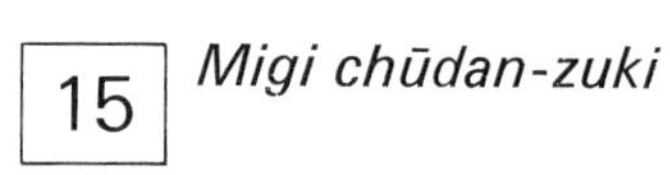

15 *Migi chūdan-zuki*

Right middle level punch

Migi ashi-dachi

Tekki 1. Kick outward, not inward. It can also be a low level kick.

Kiba-dachi

16 *Migi tekubi chūdan makiotoshi* *Hidari teishō jōdan-zuki*

Right wrist middle level twisting block/Left upper level palm heel punch Move left foot half a step toward right foot, then with left foot as pivot, slide right foot to

17 *Migi jōdan haitō uchi* *Hidari gedan teishō uchi*

Right upper level ridge hand strike/Left downward palm heel strike With right foot as pivot, rotate hips to the left. While taking the stance, execute the ridge hand

Migi zenkutsu-dachi

left diagonal front. Use a downward circular movement to execute the twisting block.

Hidari zenkutsu-dachi

strike and palm heel strike.

18 *Ryō shō jōdan kensei*

Upper level feint with both palms Pull left foot to right foot for stance. Strongly strike back of left hand against right palm. Make a slapping noise.

19 *Hidari shō gedan kokō sukui uke* *Migi shō gedan kokō tsukidashi*

Left downward tiger mouth scooping block/Right downward tiger mouth thrust Slide left foot back for stance and execute block and thrust simultaneously. Left

Heisoku-dachi

Migi zenkutsu-dachi

palm scoops outside inward and right palm thrusts downward, right palm crossing left palm. At finish, have left palm touching bottom of right elbow.

20 *Gedan awase-zuki*

Downward U punch Do Movements 19 and 20 quickly one after the other.

21 *Hidari chūdan haishu uke*

Left middle level back-hand block With right foot as pivot, rotate hips to the left to take stance facing diagonally left. Simultaneously and slowly execute the back-

Migi zenkutsu-dachi

Migi kōkutsu-dachi

hand block.

22 *Migi jōdan tate hiji-ate*

Right upper level upward elbow strike Slide right foot forward for straddle-leg stance and thrust right elbow straight up, passing it close to the right side of the

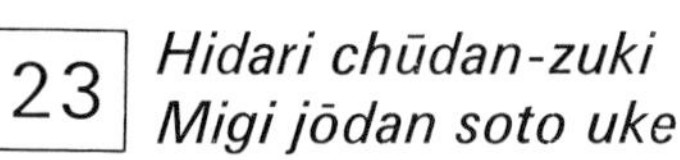

23 *Hidari chūdan-zuki* *Migi jōdan soto uke*

Left middle level punch/Right upper level outside-inward block Keeping the stance, slide feet slightly to the right while punching.

body. Bring right fist beside right ear (back of fist outward).

Kiba-dachi

24 *Migi gedan-barai Hidari ken hidari koshi*

25 *Hidari chūdan haishu uke*

Right downward block/Left fist at left side Execute the block while sliding feet well back.

Left middle level back-hand block With right

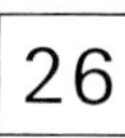

26 *Migi chūdan hiji-ate* (*Hidari shō ni ateru*)

Right middle level elbow strike (*Hit left palm*)

Migi kōkutsu-dachi

foot as pivot, rotate hips to the left for right back stance.

Kiba-dachi

26 *Migi gedan-barai*
Hidari shō migi hiji ue ni soeru

Kiba-dachi

Right downward block/Left palm at right elbow
After elbow strike, execute downward block.

27 *Hidari chūdan haishu uke*

Left middle level back-hand block With right

28 *Migi jōdan tate hiji-ate*

Right upper level upward elbow strike

Migi kōkutsu-dachi

foot as pivot, rotate hips to the right. Move left foot diagonally forward.

Kiba-dachi

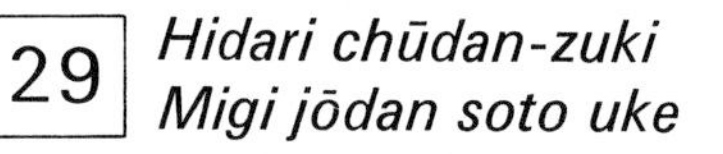

29 *Hidari chūdan-zuki* *Migi jōdan soto uke*

Left middle level punch/Right upper level outside-inward block

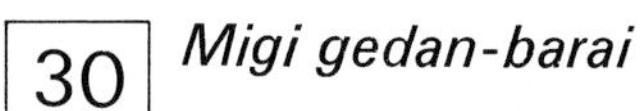

30 *Migi gedan-barai*

Right downward block

Kiba-dachi

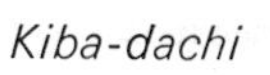

Kiba-dachi

31 *Ryō ken ryō koshi kamae*

Fists at sides of body kamae Swing both fists widely from overhead, pulling them to the sides of the body after crossing them.

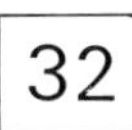

32 *Ryō ken awase-zuki (Migi ken jōdan-zuki, hidari ken chūdan-zuki)*

Hidari mae sanchin-dachi

U punch (Right fist upper level, left fist middle level)

33a *Migi tekubi chūdan makiotoshi* *Hidari teishō hidari kataguchi ni kamaeru*

Right wrist downward twisting block/Left palm heel in front of left shoulder

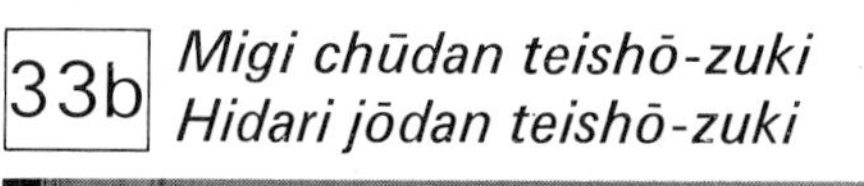

33b *Migi chūdan teishō-zuki* *Hidari jōdan teishō-zuki*

Right middle level palm heel punch/Left upper level palm heel punch

Migi mae sanchin-dachi

Migi mae sanchin-dachi

Move right foot slowly, keeping left foot in place, to return to natural position.

Shizen-tai hachinoji-dachi

Heisoku-dachi

NIJŪSHIHO: IMPORTANT POINTS

The name by which this kata is known—"twenty-four step"—came originally from the number of foot movements.

Performance of this kata is correct only when the movements are smooth and flow unbrokenly one into the other. Until total integration of varying strengths and speed are totally mastered, performance is apt to resemble a dance.

The back-hand block (*haishu uke*) used in this kata has a particular course and employs certain parts of the body in a way that clearly differentiates it from other blocks with which it should not be confused, i.e., hooking block, sword hand block, grasping block and so on.

1. Movements 1/2. In the pressing block as shown here, the left arm pulls, according to the movement of his punching arm, your opponent toward you. To counterattack, keep the back stance and slide forward for a right reverse punch. If more is needed, slide farther forward and strike his underarm with your left elbow. Alternatively, you can put your left arm under his elbow and bend it back.

2. Movement 6. When the adversary is directing his attack against your face, you can block by putting your elbows together and scissoring his arm from both sides with both wrists. You can simultaneously strike his elbow with your knee.

Another way to use the hands in this situation is to simultaneously strike his arm at different points with your fists. In either case, holding the knee up high serves the additional purpose of protecting the groin.

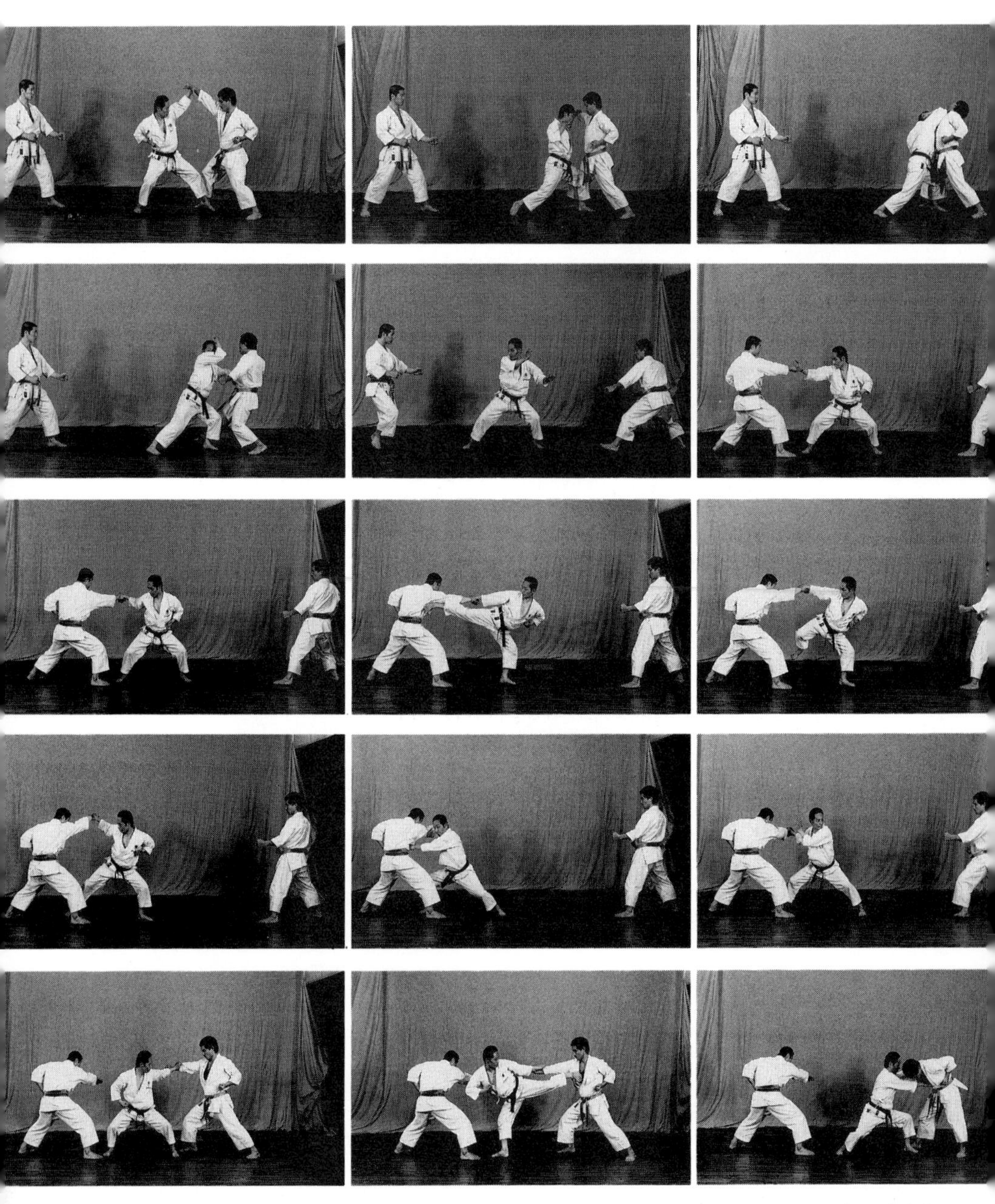

3. Movements 8/15. Against an opponent on your left, use an upper level rising block and immediately attack his face with an upward elbow strike. Rotate your hips to the right to deal with the second attacker and hook block as soon as you turn. While pulling his wrist, thrust kick to the side and follow with a left reverse punch for the finishing blow. Turning back to the left, block his wrist, pull it, and thrust kick to the side with your left foot. Follow up with a right reverse punch.

In this situation—opponents on both sides—it is important not to change the position of the hips when executing the thrust kicks.

4. Movement 16. As a continuation of the downward twisting block with the right wrist, punch downward with the right palm heel. At the same time, use the left palm heel for an attack to the face.

To be effective the course of the twist-block must be circular. Bring your right palm heel to your left side at a low level and raise it in an arc. Block by putting the back of your wrist against the back of his.

5. Movement 17. Grab your assailant's wrist with your left hand and pull it downward to get him off balance. Attack his neck or carotid artery with the sword hand or chicken wrist by swinging your right hand widely from the right side in coordination with the hip rotation. The pulling action is involved in both making him lose his balance and in your own hip rotation.

6. Movements 18/20. Clapping your hands together above your head can cause your assailant to launch a sudden and uncoordinated kicking attack. Scoop-block his leg with your left palm heel and strike his knee hard with your right palm heel. Pull up with your left hand, push down with your right. Another way is to strike his knee with your left fist and his ankle with your right.

7. Movements 21/22. After diverting your opponent's right punching fist to the side with your left back-hand, slide your right foot well forward to get between his legs. Attack his chin with a vertical elbow strike while continuing to pull his left hand to the left side to break his balance to the front. To get the correct vertically upward course of the elbow strike, bring your fist beside your ear with the back of the fist outward. If the back of the fist faces upward, there is no concentration of power.

8. Movement 33. Follow up the downward hooking block of your assailant's punch with your right wrist right away with a strike to the lower level with the right palm heel. Attack his face with the left palm heel.

It is important that the downward hooking block be coordinated with the circular movement of the right foot.

GLOSSARY

age-uke, rising block
ashi, foot, leg
ateru, strike
awase-zuki, U punch

chichi, nipple
chūdan, middle level

embusen, performance line

fudō-dachi, rooted stance
fuseru, lie flat

gedan-barai, downward block
gedan, lower level, downward
gyaku hanmi, reverse half-front facing
gyaku-zuki, reverse punch

hachinoji-dachi, open-leg stance
haishu uke, back-hand block
haitō uchi, ridge hand strike
hasami uke, scissors block
heisoku-dachi, feet-together stance
hidari, left
hiji, elbow
hiji ate, elbow strike
hineri uke, twisting block
hiraki, open
hitosashiyubi, index finger
hiza, knee

ikken hissatsu, to kill with one blow
ippon nukite, one-knuckle spear hand
ittan, once

jōdan, upper level
jōtai, upper body

kahō, downward
kaikomu, fold
kake shutō uke, hooking sword hand block
kakiwake, reverse wedge
kamae, posture, position
kamaeru, take a posture
kata, shoulder
kataguchi, shoulder
keage, snap kick
keitō, chicken-head wrist
kekomi, thrust kick
kensei, feint
keru, kick
kiba-dachi, straddle-leg stance
kime, decide
kō, back of hand
kōhō, back direction
kokō, tiger mouth
kōkutsu-dachi, back stance
koshi, hip

mae, before, in front of
mae-geri, front kick
makiotoshi, twist-fall
mawashi-geri, roundhouse kick
migi, right
mikazuki-geri, crescent kick
muki, facing
mune, chest
musubi-dachi, informal attention stance, toes out

naiwan, inner side of forearm
nami-gaeshi, returning wave kick
naname, diagonally
narabe, put side by side
neko ashi-dachi, cat leg stance
nobasu, extend
nukite, spear hand

oi-zuki, lunge punch
osae-uke, pressing block
oshidasu, push out

ryō, both

saki, beyond
sanchin-dachi, hourglass stance
sayū, left and right, both sides
seiryūtō, ox jaw hand
seiryūtō-zuki, ox-jaw hand punch

shisei, posture
shita, down
shizen-tai, natural position
shōmon, front
shō, palm
soeru, attach
sokumen, side
sono mama, as it is
soto uke, outside-inward block
sukoshi, a little
sukui uke, scooping block
sun, unit of length, about three centimeters
sun-dome, to arrest a technique just before making contact

tanden, center of gravity
tate hiji-ate, vertical elbow strike
tate shutō uke, vertical sword hand block
te, hand
teishō, palm-heel
tekubi, wrist
tsukamiyose, grasping-pulling
tsukidashi, thrust
tsumasaki, toe tip

uchi, strike
uchi uke, inside-outward block
ue, above, on top of
uke, block
uke-zuki, block-punch
uraken uchi, back-fist strike
ura-zuki, close punch
ushiro, back, rear

yoko, side
yoko uke, side block
yori, more than

zenkutsu-dachi, front stance

JAPANESE SPIRITUALITY

BUSHIDO The Soul of Japan *Inazo Nitobe*

Written specifically for a Western audience in 1900 by Japan's under-secretary general to the League of Nations, Bushido explains concepts such as honor and loyalty within traditional Japanese ethics. The book is a classic, and as such throws a great deal of light on Japanese thinking and behavior, both past and present.

Hardcover, 160 pages, ISBN 978-1-56836-440-7

MUSASHI An Epic Novel of the Samurai Era *Eiji Yoshikawa*

This classic work tells of the legendary samurai who was the greatest swordsman of all time. "... a stirring saga... one that will prove popular not only for readers interested in Japan but also for those who simply want a rousing read."—*The Washington Post*

Hardcover, 978 pages, ISBN 978-1-56836-427-8

SEPPUKU A History of Samurai Suicide *Andrew Rankin*

A collection of thrilling samurai tales tracing the history of seppuku from ancient times to the twentieth century.

Softcover, 256 pages, ISBN 978-1-56836-586-2

EAT SLEEP SIT My Year at Japan's Most Rigorous Zen Temple *Kaoru Nonomura*

The true story of one ordinary man's search for meaning to life at Japan's strictest Zen Temple.

Paperback, 328 pages, ISBN 978-1-56836-565-7

THE ESSENCE OF SHINTO Japan's Spiritual Heart *Motohisa Yamakage*

The author explains the core values of Shinto, as well as exploring the very profound aspects of the original Shinto of ancient times. He also carefully analyzes the relationships of the spirit and soul, which will provide readers with informed and invaluable insight into how spirituality affects our daily existence.

Hardcover, 232 pages, ISBN 978-1-56836-437-7

THE TWENTY GUIDING PRINCIPLES OF KARATE

The Spiritual Legacy of the Master *Gichin Funakoshi*

Gichin Funakoshi, "the father of karate," penned his now legendary twenty principles more than 60 years ago. While the principles have circulated for years, a translation of the accompanying commentary has never found its way into publication—until now.

Hardcover, 128 pages, ISBN 978-1-56836-496-4

MIND OVER MUSCLE Writings from the Founder of Judo *Jigoro Kano*

In 1882 Jigoro Kano founded Kodokan Judo in Tokyo. This book is a collection of the essential teachings by the founder, selected and compiled from his wealth of writings and lectures spanning a period of fifty-one years. Throughout his life, Kano repeatedly emphasized grasping the correct meaning of judo and putting it into practice.

Hardcover, 160 pages, ISBN 978-1-56836-497-1